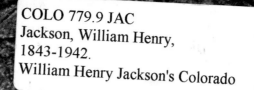

William Henry Jackson's
COLORADO

William Henry Jackson's
COLORADO

Compiled by

William C. Jones and Elizabeth B. Jones

Foreword by

Marshall Sprague

PRUETT **P** PUBLISHING COMPANY
Boulder, Colorado

ISBN: 0-87108-092-3 (Regular Edition)

1   2   3   4   5   6   7   8   9

49376 11/76 pub. 28.00

Library of Congress Cataloging in Publication Data

Jackson, William Henry, 1843-1942.
   William Henry Jackson's Colorado.

   1. Photography, Artistic. 2. Colorado--Description
and travel--Views. 3. Jackson, William Henry,
1843-1942. I. Jones, William C., 1937-
II. Jones, Elizabeth B., 1942-   III. Title.
TR652.J3 1975   779'.9'97880924   75-33046

Printed in the U.S.A.

Acknowledgments

In compiling this book, a most difficult task was that of selecting two hundred photos from among the several thousand, representing the work of William Henry Jackson in Colorado. The accomplishment of this objective was made possible through the generous help provided by several individuals and institutions, including Augie Mastrogiuseppe, photographic librarian of the Western History Department of the Denver Public Library; Robert W. Richardson, Executive Director of the Colorado Railroad Museum; Terry Mangan and Christopher Compton, both former librarians in the Documentary Resources Department of the State Historical Society of Colorado, and the staff of the Photographic Library, United States Geological Survey, Denver Federal Center.

We are further indebted to Mr. Mastrogiuseppe for his generous aid in identifying the locations and subjects of a number of photographs, as well as for his expertise in perusing and verifying the collection selected for this book.

We wish to thank the staff of the Pruett Publishing Company for its efforts in the production and publication of this book.

Photographs were furnished through the courtesy of the following institutions:

Western History Department, Denver Public Library for photos on pages ii, vi, xii, 58, 63, 68, 112, 113, 127, 172

Colorado Railroad Museum for photos on pages 76, 89 (bottom), 102, 103, 104, 106, 107, 108, 109

United States Geological Survey for photos on pages xvii, xx, 8, 9, 17, 19, 24, 34 (bottom), 39, 67 (bottom), 149 (bottom), 164 (bottom)

The State Historical Society of Colorado for all photos not otherwise credited to any of the above sources.

The color prints found on the jacket and endpapers are typical of those sold by the Detroit Publishing Company, beginning in 1898. They were produced by hand-coloring black and white photographs, which were subsequently reproduced by what was known as the photochrom process.

William C. Jones
Elizabeth B. Jones
Arvada, Colorado, 1975

The studio of the W.H. Jackson Photographic Co. in Denver about 1890. Second from right is L.C. McClure, later a prominent Denver photographer

Contents

William Henry Jackson celebrates his 99th birthday at the New York Explorers' Club

Foreword

The words "mountain men" bring to mind Kit Carson and Jim Bridger and the other great ones of the fur trade era. But we have here a different kind of mountain man whose achievements were at least equal to those of the earlier trail blazers. William Henry Jackson was the finest of the nation's wet-plate photographers.

If anyone else saw more of the American West than Jackson, there is no record of it. If anyone else risked his neck as often as he did to see that West from every possible and impossible angle, there is no record of that either. Jackson was incredible, and so are a great many of the eighty thousand photos that he took of the Rockies, including the Colorado samples in this book.

There is no clue as to why he grew up thinking pictures, scene, tension, composition, instead of the way you and I think. He was born on a farm in New York in 1843, and he died in New York ninety-nine years later, soon after reading galleys on a very lively book about — guess what? — photography called *Time Exposure*. In between was enough living for ten men, starting in Troy, New York, at the age of fifteen, as one of those sleight-of-hand craftsmen who touch up photos to make ugly people look handsome.

What gets me is how he survived it all — scrambling around those thousands of precipices; those fourteen-thousand-foot Colorado peaks jangling with electricity; those great waterfalls; and getting caught in those sudden violent hail-and-wind storms above timberline that can kill a hiker in a matter of minutes.

Jackson was a smallish man and neatly assembled, like an otter. He had the endurance of a bobcat and the easy balance and spring of a bighorn sheep. No mountaineer knew more than he about how to keep alive and comfortable in the wilderness. No prospector knew more about the subtle business of making horses and mules happy. His riding mare Dolly had to be treated with particular reverence as she was a queenly and disdainful creature who considered herself far superior, socially, to the pack mule Old Molly and even to the famous indispensable Hypo who carried Jackson's dark-box and bath-holder.

Jackson understood people as well as animals. General Palmer, founder of the Denver and Rio Grande Railroad, detested snooping cameramen, but he permitted Jackson to photograph whatever caught his eye, in Palmer's secret Gen Eyrie castle near the Garden of the Gods. Jackson also had a special sympathy for, and appreciation of, the Indians. It was this sympathy that caused the Uncompahgre Utes at Los Pinos Agency to allow themselves to be photographed for the first time.

His magnificent portrait of Chief Ouray stands in a class by itself.

The most spectacular of the Jackson photos were those taken in Colorado during the 1870's, under the direction of that topographical genius, Ferdinand V. Hayden, for the U.S. Geological and Geographical Surveys of the Territories. Hayden was the scientific force behind that epical project, but Jackson was the promotion man who brought Hayden's work to world-wide attention. His photos of Two-Story House in present Mesa Verde National Park gave people their first knowledge of the Basket Maker civilizations that flourished in those fascinating dwellings a thousand years ago.

The whole nation was thrilled by the story of how Jackson and the imperturbable Hypo survived a freezing night on Notch Mountain above Eagle River waiting for the clouds to clear so that he could photograph the Mount of the Holy Cross, "culminating," as James Gardner wrote at the time, "in a dark precipice 3,000 feet high on which rests the great White Cross 1,500 feet long — as perfect in form as you can imagine." This dramatic picture has come to be regarded as the most celebrated mountain photograph ever made. And then there was Jackson's phenomenal shot of the highest Saguache Range spreading away from his camera, perched on the summit of La Plata Peak above Leadville. The Jackson panorama of Central City with the Teller House in the center still remains the standard post card picture.

The explorations of Zebulon Pike, Stephen Long and John Charles Fremont gave Americans some idea of the Colorado Rockies, and a bit later tens of thousands were lured to those mountains by gold and silver. We can only guess how many millions have come during the past century to see for themselves if Jackson told the truth in his pictures. And since his pictures are timeless, we have every reason to expect that many more millions will be drawn by them to Colorado in the century ahead.

Marshall Sprague
Colorado Springs, Colorado

Photography in Jackson's Era

Photography in the 1870's and 1880's was a far cry from the convenience of today. In that era, a procedure known as the "wet plate" process was in general use. It was complicated and chancy and required speed and efficiency. The photographer could not afford to be more than thirty minutes from a darkroom. As one can see, this created problems for a roving explorer like W. H. Jackson.

When the photographic unit was traveling, Jackson brought cameras to accommodate several sizes of glass plates including a 5 x 8 inch, an 11 x 14 inch, a stereoscopic size to produce the then popular three dimensional pictures (called stereopticon), and on some trips a giant 20 x 24 inch size. A wide variety of supplies were required including collodion, silver nitrate and iron sulphate, along with a portable dark room. Since the art of enlargement had not yet been introduced, large cameras and plates had to be used to bring out the details of a particularly impressive scene and to permit the production of large prints. Such equipment was not necessary when making portraits and less dramatic scenes not desired in large print sizes. The darkroom, barely large enough for Jackson to enter, was made of canvas arranged over a folding tripod and lined with orange calico because of its ability to filter certain light rays.

The procedure followed by Jackson was awkward and complicated. After locating the desired view, the pack mule was brought as close as possible. The camera(s) were then set up and the tent darkroom erected and made light-proof. The plates to be exposed were washed with collodion, immersed in the silver bath and placed in a holder ready for exposure. Following the exposure, Jackson returned to the darkroom where he flooded the plate with developing fluid, "fixed" it with cyanide solution, washed the plate again and allowed it to dry before packing. Back at camp the plate was varnished and carefully packed for shipment to the studio where it was placed over paper coated with common salt and albumin to produce a print. This was often done on the roof to utilize sunlight; thus the term solar prints.

It is obvious that the bulk with which Jackson was forced to travel (an estimated three hundred pounds), presented many problems. On a few occasions the mules retaliated by rolling over on their heavy burdens, or by slipping a pack, both actions costing valuable exposed plates and lost time as Jackson tried to recapture specific shots. Sometimes the mules were physically unable to carry the heavy burdens over the terrain, forcing the men to take some of the load. Jackson attempted to circumvent the problem of bulk in 1877, on a trip to the Southwest. A new dry film was being introduced and after successful experiments, he decided to take only his 8 x 10 camera and the new film. Upon returning to Washington, try as he might, not one of the four hundred exposures produced a print. A complete failure! Thoroughly disappointed, Jackson attributed the debacle to the long interval between exposure and development. By the 1890's Eastman Kodak was marketing the new celluloid film, the forerunner of modern photography and one can imagine Jackson's reluctance to use this new method until proven to be reliable.

Most of Jackson's photographs were assigned a title and number, and these along with the company name, appeared on all prints. This provided easy reference and protection against pirating. Throughout this book, these original titles have been utilized with only minor changes for clarity. Certain place names may be unfamiliar due to changes which have occurred, such as the renaming of the Grand River in 1921, to the Colorado River.

Many advances have been made in photography since Jackson and his fellow professionals developed their first plates, but rare is the photographer today who can excel the magnificence produced through those "magic boxes". In spite of the bulbous size of the cameras, indeed because of it, they were able to produce panoramas in such detail as to give the viewer the feeling of standing on the brink of the Rocky Mountains. We are fortunate that men like Jackson were willing to forsake the comfort of a studio in favor of the beautiful but temperamental high and far places.

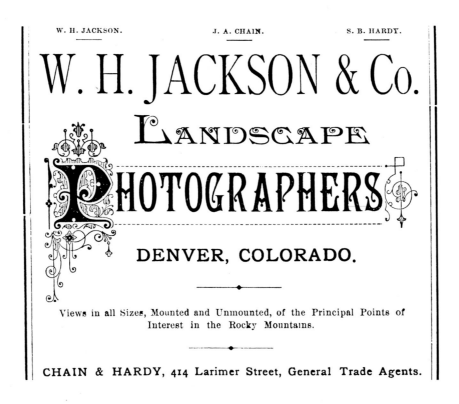

W. H. JACKSON. J. A. CHAIN. S. B. HARDY.

W. H. JACKSON & Co.
LANDSCAPE
PHOTOGRAPHERS

DENVER, COLORADO.

Views in all Sizes, Mounted and Unmounted, of the Principal Points of Interest in the Rocky Mountains.

CHAIN & HARDY, 414 Larimer Street, General Trade Agents.

Introduction

When William Henry Jackson was born in 1843, the area that would eventually become the Centennial State of Colorado, was claimed as part of Mexico, Texas and the United States. At his death on June 30, 1942, Colorado had not only achieved statehood, but was the regional leader in commerce, finance and industry, and during that war year, was the center for various military activities. Jackson was a witness to much of that change, but his interest in Colorado was predominantly in the natural beauty which has become the state's major attraction for residents and visitors alike.

This book focuses on only one facet of Jackson's extensive photographic explorations, for the pioneer photographer was not limited to the confines of the Colorado Rockies, but many times took his camera throughout the United States, to Mexico, and on his most unusual trip, into Europe and Asia. Colorado, however, remained his favorite area and after making several trips between 1870 and 1879, he decided to locate his photographic studio in Denver, the more readily to explore and photograph the nearby Rockies. Even after moving to Detroit and later to New York City, Jackson returned to Colorado many times.

Thanks to Jackson's pioneering spirit we can appreciate the scenes of nature as they waited in regal silence for the strident noise of man. We can see pictures of towns, long since dead, at the height of their lively existence. We can watch and almost hear as America moves West by lumbering Prairie Schooner, bone-jostling stage coaches, and the clamorous steam train. We can reflect on the countenance of the Indians who once roamed freely, but who, by Jackson's time, were being confined to sections of land they neither found desirable, nor in some cases, bearable. All of this we have as the living record of one man's work of preserving his era for all posterity to enjoy.

Born in Keeseville, New York, on April 4, 1843, the eldest of seven children, Jackson spent his first twenty years leading a rather ordinary life. Notwithstanding, even as a youngster, he showed promise as a recorder and observer, demonstrating a propensity for sketching accounts of events and activities.

Jackson's initial exposure to the neo-science of photography came at the age of fifteen when he went to work as a touch-up artist for C. C. Schoonmaker's studio in Troy, New York. The result was a fascination for the "image box" that never faded during the remainder of his ninety-nine years.

After moving to Rutland, Vermont, Jackson began working for a local photographer painting backgrounds and adding the finishing touches to portraits. This training, together with experience in painting advertising and campaign signs, helped to develop his sense of photography as an art medium.

In 1862, Jackson enlisted in the Second Vermont Brigade and although he did not see front line action in the Civil War, he was kept busy as the official staff artist depicting camp and military life. These sketches not only provided information for military records, but were informative to those waiting back home. His enlistment ended in June, 1863, at which time he returned home to Rutland amid great family rejoicing.

After settling down to a routine, Jackson was offered a position in Burlington, Vermont, with Styles' "Gallery of Art" early in 1865. Considering that the move would benefit his career, he decided to accept the offer, but it was to prove short lived. After the excitement of military life, the tedium of studio routine weighted heavily on Jackson and the call of the adventurous West was growing with each passing day. The necessary catalyst for change, a romantic break-up with his sweetheart, provided the impetus needed to pick up and begin his move toward the West. Although the move promised much hardship, Jackson in later years, never regretted making the decision which in June, 1866, found him with two friends in Nebraska City, Nebraska Territory, newly signed on with a supply train headed for the silver mines of Virginia City, Montana. Jackson, the budding artist and would-be photographer, had signed on as a bullwhacker. Enroute he changed his mind and joined a wagon train bound for Salt Lake City, from where he eventually moved to Los Angeles in December, 1866.

Intent now on joining the California gold rush, Jackson started north, often doing ranch work to earn meals and transportation. But the lure of the gold fields had been tempered by the hard crucible of the frontier and he began to yearn for home. After securing transportation back to Los Angeles, he signed on in April with a crew taking wild horses to Omaha.

After a long, perilous and bitter trip, Jackson arrived in Julesburg, Colorado, on July 30, 1867, and continued to Omaha via the Union Pacific. For four months of grueling work, Jackson received the sum total of twenty dollars, and that was given grudgingly.

With this "vast" sum in his pocket and fame and fortune far from made, Jackson elected to stay in Omaha and went to work for one of the city's two photographers. As his photographic ability improved, a loan from his father together with his own capital, enabled him to buy out not only his employer but also the competition. So it was that Jackson became known as W. H. Jackson, photographer. In 1868, together with his two brothers Fred and Ed, they established Jackson Brothers Studio.

Jackson stuck to studio work and concentrated on building up a trade. Through churches, social groups and political clubs, he developed a regular clientele for portraits. Occasionally Jackson would take brief trips to the nearby Indian camps, making portraits to add to his rapidly growing western collection.

While the entire nation watched breathlessly as the Union Pacific and Central Pacific railroads raced to form the nation's first transcontinental railroad, Jackson was lamenting the fact that his business was not big enough to allow him to free lance along the line to Promontory, Utah, the agreed meeting place of the two giants. Business was not the only reason he could not pursue the tracks West. On May 10, 1869, the same day the golden spike was driven at Promontory Point, Jackson married Mollie Greer, a lovely lady who was almost as enthusiastic about his work as the photographer himself.

About the time of their marriage, Jackson received an order from the Union Pacific for pictures along the line to Utah. Following a honeymoon aboard a Missouri River steamboat to St. Louis, Jackson put his new bride on a train bound for her family in Ohio and then headed west to begin several months of photographic work for the railroad.

Jackson now believed he could establish a profession as a scenic photographer. Although this brought little income, Jackson and his assistants managed to make their way West, trading pictures for passage on trains and for their meals. It was July when Jackson finally photographed Promontory Point, Utah. This trip was significant because it was his first step as a commercial photographer and because the products of this trip laid the foundation for future trips.

Throughout the winter of 1869, Jackson Brothers Studio was reaping the benefits of the past summer's adventures and as the summer of 1870 approached, there was anticipation of new targets for exposure. In July, Dr. Ferdinand Vandiveer Hayden, head geologist of the United States Geological Survey, arrived in Omaha and offered Jackson a position with the survey team heading for Wyoming.

After arranging for the management of the studio, Jackson left for Cheyenne on August 1, 1870, to join the first Hayden Survey team. He had already seen most of the country to be surveyed but this time he was exploring and photographing the hidden side of hills he had already seen from a distance. Near the end of the 1870 survey, Hayden requested Jackson to detour to the Pike's Peak region for the photographer's first trip to Colorado, aside from his brief stop at Julesburg in 1867. After completing his assignment in Colorado, he headed for Washington, D.C., to join with Hayden in planning for the next summer's expedition. Jackson decided that since he was employed by the government, it was only wise to sell his studio in Omaha. However, since buyers were scarce and his brothers had dropped from the partnership, Mollie managed the business during the 1871 survey.

The team left Ogden June 10, 1871, with specific designs to study and record the phenomenon known as Coulter's Hell. Jackson was a key figure in this trip since quite a controversy had grown up around the actual existence of boiling pots and belching geysers! Pictures were essential for the people seeking to preserve the area. Thanks to Jackson's work and Hayden's lobbying, Congress began considering the nation's first national park in December, 1871. A beautifully bound file of Jackson's photos of the area was presented to each member of Congress and the work was apparently so impressive that Congress, without one dissenting vote, created Yellowstone National Park. The bill became law when signed by President Grant on March 1, 1872.

Congress generously appropriated additional funds for the 1872 survey to be used for further exploration of Yellowstone Park and the Teton Range. Jackson's dedication to his job this time was therapeutic as well as professional, for his wife Mollie, had died earlier that year in childbirth. Starting from Ogden, the party surveyed the spectacular Teton Range. Challenged by steep narrow winding ledges encrusted in ice, Jackson earned every dime paid him by the government.

The next survey was again aimed at the Northwest, but Indian trouble in Wyoming precluded any trips in that direction. As an alternative, Hayden elected to explore the Colorado Rockies. Because of the expanse of the area, the survey team was split into several small groups. Jackson's photographic unit was assigned the heady responsibility of exploring scenic features from Long's Peak south to Gray's and Torrey's Peaks, then to Fairplay where they were to meet the rest of the survey team.

After the reunion, Hayden set out in search of the much talked about Mount of the Holy Cross, a mountain peak reputed to have a cross of snow inscribed on its face. The locating of this peak and Jackson's superb photographs of the snowy cross, brought Jackson and the Hayden Survey considerable fame and prestige. September 4th found the team back in Denver already planning for the survey of 1874.

Jackson interrupted his busy work schedule that autumn to become married on October 8th, to Emilie Painter, a cousin of William Gilpin, the first Territorial Governor of Colorado.

The nation was still feeling the effects of the panic of 1873, and Congress delayed appropriating any money for the 1874 survey until the end of July. Most of the survey team members were waiting at their camp near Clear Creek, west of Denver, when orders arrived to proceed. The photographic unit headed directly for Berthoud Pass, then through Middle and South Parks, on to Poncha Pass and through the San Luis Valley. The main objectives of this expedition were to contact the Uncompahgre Utes at Los Pinos Agency and to tour Baker's Park in the San Juan Mountains.

While en route to Baker's Park, Jackson met an acquaintance from Omaha, E. H. Cooper, who together with John Moss, subsequently led the photographic unit to the Indian ruins in Mancos Canyon, now a part of Mesa Verde National Park. Winter had almost closed in on the team by the time they finished their sometime planned and sometime spontaneous photography, and on October 14th Jackson headed for Denver, already contemplating his next summer's trip, which he hoped would bring a return to southwestern Colorado.

1875 found the photographic section busy at work among the ruins of the Southwest. Not only in Colorado, but also in Utah, New Mexico and Arizona. Among the most friendly Indians encountered on this trip were the Hopi, who not only posed for Jackson's camera but warmly and graciously welcomed the team into their homes. Jackson and the party did, however, have problems with the Paiute Indians who caused them tense moments with serious heckling and threats.

Rendezvous of the Hayden Survey party in the spring of 1873, on Clear Creek, four miles northwest of Denver

Dr. Hayden, left, and several members of the survey party pose for Jackson during the 1873 expedition

During the national centennial of 1876, Jackson was in Philadelphia representing the Geological Survey. His exhibit consisted of clay replicas of portions of the Indian ruins he had photographed and for which he was awarded a bronze medal. After all the distraction of a busy city, he longed for the solitude of the open spaces.

In 1877, Jackson decided to strike for the Southwest, independent of the Hayden Survey which was headed for Wyoming and Montana. Photographically, the effort was a disaster. A new dry film process, claiming to hold the image for unlimited time, proved to be less than satisfactory: of four hundred exposures not a single one could be developed.

The Hayden Survey of 1878, was again directed to Wyoming and Montana. This proved to be Jackson's last trip with the Geological Survey, because in 1879, Congress changed the structure of the survey, eliminating funds for the photographic unit. Momentarily caught off guard, Jackson reacted quickly and decided to move to Denver to open his own studio. The W. H. Jackson Photographic Company opened its door at 413 Larimer Street in the fall of 1879.

While in Colorado, Jackson took many splendid pictures throughout the state and surrounding regions. Some of his best customers were the railroads which hired him to photograph their lines for advertising as well as for their own information. The by-product of this work was a wealth of beautiful scenic pictures for the enjoyment of future generations. Among his out-of-state trips were those to the Grand Canyon of the Colorado, Mexico, and along the lines of the Baltimore and Ohio Railroad. The most unusual trip Jackson engaged in was for the World Transportation Commission, commissioned by the Columbian Museum to study foreign railroads and transportation. The expedition lasted seventeen months during 1893 and 1894, and took him to Europe, Africa, Australia and Asia, and even included a tour of the wilderness of Siberia in northern Russia.

In 1897, Jackson's company, by then known as the W. H. Jackson Photographic and Publishing Company, was purchased by the Photochrom Company, itself a part of the Detroit Publishing Company. Jackson was made a director of the firm and in early 1898, moved his family to Detroit. From Detroit, Jackson continued to explore the wonders of this great nation. His travels took him to the Black Hills of South Dakota, California, Illinois and Massachusetts. Many summers were spent in Colorado as he continued to explore the state in which he had taken many of his most memorable photographs.

The Detroit Publishing Company went into receivership in 1924, and Jackson, now eighty-one, again found himself unemployed. Still a dapper gentleman, he moved to Washington, D.C., for a time, then to New York City to work as a research secretary for the Oregon Trail Memorial Association. In 1935, he was commissioned to paint a series of murals for the Department of the Interior, depicting early days on the Geological Surveys. In these later years, Jackson became almost as widely known for his western paintings as for his photographic accomplishments.

The old picture maker was never satisfied to sit peacefully and contemplate his long life and the adventures he had experienced. He continued to travel to Michigan, Colorado, Washington, California and Wyoming, in general simply to enjoy the country. In 1937, while in Cheyenne, Jackson fractured several vertebrae when he fell on his back. The ninety-four year old pioneer recovered fully, although lamenting that he was unable to ride horses!

Various organizations were beginning to pay tribute to Jackson. In 1937, he received a medal from the University of Colorado in recognition of his years of public service. The following year, he was made an honorary member of the Royal Photographic Society of Great Britain. In 1939, he received an honorary membership in the American Alpine Club and that same year the Oregon Trail Association's publication carried a complete series of his paintings which focused on his 1866 journey along the Oregon Trail. In 1940, Jackson published his autobiography, *Time Exposure,* relating the colorful details of his ninety-seven years. In 1941, he received an honorary Doctor of Law Degree from the University of Wyoming, a fitting tribute in the twilight of his years.

William Henry Jackson, residing in New York City, died on Tuesday, June 30, 1942, at the age of ninety-nine years. According to newspaper accounts, he succumbed to injuries suffered in a fall the previous Friday. The legacy which he left to his country is incalculable even by today's standards. Estimates of his total accumulation of photographic negatives is conservatively set at 80,000. What Jackson did in Colorado is only a sample of what he did throughout the nation and the world. Without his extensive picture coverage of the northwestern Wyoming region, there might never have been a Yellowstone or Teton National Park. Mesa Verde might have been forever lost to marauding man if publicity from Jackson's pictures had not spurred officials into action. Turn of the century scenes of the mysterious East would have gone unrecorded had he not journeyed to Asia. All of this and much more, would have been forever lost had it not been for this Pioneer Photographer and his third eye.

On Argentine Pass with the portable darkroom — 1873

High and Far Places

The majesty of towering mountain peaks, gaping canyons, placid parks and meadows, eroded and contorted rocks, provide a magnificent natural backdrop for an exploring photographer. Through frequent trips, Jackson accumulated a great volume of photographic plates of Colorado. While it is generally impossible to specifically date most pictures, there are two instances, recorded by Jackson in his diaries, for which dating is possible: the United States Geological Survey expeditions of 1873 and 1874.

Following his first brief trip to Colorado in 1870, Jackson was convinced of the necessity for further surveys. His opportunity came in 1873, when Ferdinand Vandiveer Hayden, in charge of the U.S. Geological Survey, appointed him head of the photographic unit and directed him to explore the areas of Long's Peak, Gray's and Torrey's Peaks and, finally, Fairplay where the various other units of the survey were to unite. On August 19, 1873, the entire Hayden Survey team crossed Tennessee Pass to the headwaters of the Eagle River. The objective of this trip was to survey the elusive Mount of the Holy Cross. Prior to 1873, rumors circulated throughout the country, particularly in the West, about this phenomenon of nature — a mountain with a cross of snow etched on its face. Most reports were from secondary sources and a few eyewitness accounts, but there had been no tangible evidence submitted to prove its existence. Hayden ordered the photographic unit to scale Notch Mountain and attempt pictures of the Mount from across the valley. The ascent was hampered by miserable weather and the awkward equipment. Following a bitter cold, wet night with little shelter and no food or water, Jackson was rewarded by a brief but memorable exposure of the snowy cross through the clouds. Years later, Jackson stated that of the pictures he was to take of the Mount in succeeding years, none surpassed the first exposure on August 24, 1873.

The Hayden Survey of 1874, left Denver on July 21st, heading for Berthoud Pass and a route through Middle and South Parks, down the San Luis Valley to the Los Pinos Indian Agency and on to Baker's Park. On the way to Baker's Park, Jackson met an old acquaintance who eventually led the photographic unit on the first exploration of Mancos Canyon and to other ruins in the Southwest.

The result of these trips was a collection of pictures showing the magnificence of the Colorado landscape, previously known only to Indian tribes and a few adventurous frontiersmen. Succeeding generations will owe a debt to Jackson for leaving a memory of the massive splendor of nature touched only by the wind.

Garden of the Gods, the Seal and Bear

Garden of the Gods, the Three Graces

Garden of the Gods, Cathedral Spires

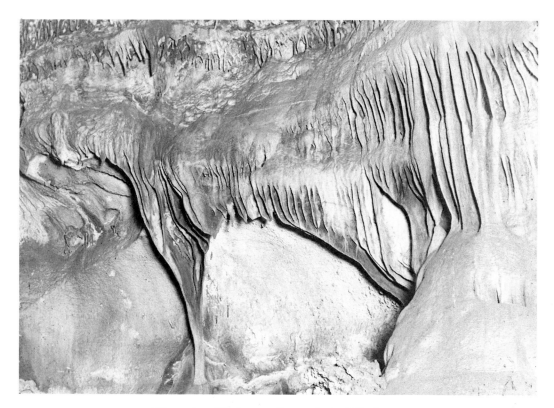

Mastodon Skeleton, Cave of the Winds

Horse-shoe Tunnel, Cave of the Winds

Crossing timberline, Manitou & Pike's Peak Ry.

Pike's Peak — a snowstorm on the summit

Palmer Lake, looking northeast — 1874

Camp by rock monument near Kountz, Douglas County — 1870

Eroded Sandstones, Monument Park — 1873

Nederland Park near Boulder

The Continental Divide on Rollins Pass, Denver, Northwestern & Pacific Ry.

Gray's and Torrey's Peaks

Berthoud Pass — 1874

14

The Crater, Long's Peak

Long's Peak from Estes Park

Herman's cabin on Grand Lake — 1874

Middle Park, looking north across the Grand River, from the mouth of the Blue River — 1874

Eagle River Canon, Denver & Rio Grande Ry.

Entrance to the Canon of the Grand (Gore Canyon) — 1874

The walls of the Canon of the Grand River (Glenwood Canyon)

Second tunnel in the Canon of the Grand River (Glenwood Canyon)

Canon of the Grand (Glenwood Canyon) looking west towards Glenwood Springs

The Grand River and Sopris Peak from Glenwood Springs

Maroon Peaks near Aspen

The Seven Castles, Colorado Midland Ry.

View over the summits of the Sawatch Range -— 1873

26

Mt. Massive from Hagerman Tunnel, Colorado Midland Railway

Red Cliff Canyon, Denver & Rio Grande Ry.

Loch Ivanhoe on the Colorado Midland Ry.

Hell Gate, Colorado Midland Ry.

First glimpse of the Holy Cross, Clarence Jackson in center — 1893

Mount of the Holy Cross — 1893

There is a mountain in the
      distant West
That, sun-defying, in its
      deep ravines
Displays a cross of snow
      upon its side. — Longfellow

In a career of countless photographic "firsts," there was no more memorable accomplishment than Jackson's photographs of the Mount of the Holy Cross. The peak was located during the 1873 Hayden Survey in response to countless rumors of its existence amid little real proof. After a long and difficult climb on August 23rd, the snowy cross was captured on Jackson's glass plates on the morning of August 24, 1873, exactly as seen on the preceding pages. To simulate the manner in which the clouds parted to reveal the cross, a composite photo was made, using clouds photographed in Denver. Twenty years later Jackson returned with his son Clarence, to again capture the scene as viewed by the original party.

Mt. Elbert from Leadville

Upper Twin Lake — 1873

Mt. Princeton from near Buena Vista

Lake Brennam

Mt. Antero from Hayward Springs

The Spanish Peaks

Mt. Harvard and the Valley of the Arkansas

Bird's-eye view, Black Canon of the Gunnison

The Rio Grande River at Wagon Wheel Gap

Curecanti Needle in the Black Canon of the Gunnison

Uncompahgre Peak

San Miguel Valley from Pandora

Mt. Sneffles from Dallas Divide

Bridal Veil Falls near Telluride

Trout Lake, along the Rio Grande Southern Ry.

Mount Wilson from Ophir Pass

Lake San Cristoval near Lake City

Sunshine Peak from Illium Curve, Rio Grande Southern Ry.

Baker's Park from Howardsville

Sultan Mountain

Elk Park and Garfield Peak, Denver & Rio Grande Ry.

Needle Mountains from Animas Canyon

Colorado's First Citizens

The purpose of photography has been to capture portraits, natural settings and events for timeless reference. One of William Henry Jackson's projects was to record the physical essence of the tribes of American Indians so as to preserve at least their costume, if not their heritage. He had a degree of success in Nebraska, Wyoming, Montana, even in Mexico. The Colorado Utes, however, proved to be less than cooperative.

When visiting the Los Pinos Indian Agency during the 1874 Hayden Survey, Jackson at first experienced success with the Uncompahgre Ute Chief, Ouray and his wife Chipeta both being willing subjects. Even Sub-Chief Peah at first posed in full regalia, but because of dire predictions by the medicine man, the tribe became hostile, not so much toward Jackson as his "magic box". Unwilling to create an incident, the photographic team made a reluctant but expeditious departure.

The most spectacular event of the 1874 trip was the discovery of the ancient cliff dwellings of Mancos Canyon. Jackson spent several days in the southwestern part of Colorado photographing these ruins, long since deserted by their builders. Much of who these people were, where they came from, why they left and where they went, remains a mystery even today, although it has been theorized that a prolonged drought caused the inhabitants to leave the area and to be assimilated with tribes to the south. Jackson's photos attest to the fact that they were much more than nomads, once thought to be the sole occupants of the land. These people were city dwellers. Had the Survey party elected to follow another canyon they, not Richard Wetherill, would have discovered the diamond of the collection: the magnificent Cliff Palace. After its discovery in 1888, Jackson returned to the area to capture another photographic first. However, in 1874, Jackson elected to push along to McElmo Creek, investigating ruins between there and Hovenweep Creek, including the Hovenweep ruins on the Colorado-Utah border.

During the National Centennial of 1876, Jackson received recognition for his camera work on the cliff dwellings and also a commendation for a replica of the cliff dwellings, which he had constructed to demonstrate to the people of America the marvelous finds and the value of such activities by the United States Geological Survey.

Jackson's photographs played an important role in persuading the Congress to establish Mesa Verde National Park in 1906, thus forever preserving the remains of Colorado's first cities.

The first photograph of Mesa Verde — Two-Story House in Mancos Canon
— September 10, 1874, John Moss, left, and Ernest Ingersoll

Mesa Verde — Cliff Palace from across the canyon

Jackson's Diary for September 9, 1874

...down & in some instances larger masses
of rock had become separated & removed
from the main mass, & thus dividing
the walls.

As evening approached we made
our camp under a little bunch of
cedars & beneath the highest walls
of the canon. Hed found nothing
that really came up to my idea of
the grand or picturesque for
photo's & began to feel a little doubtful
& discouraged. All hands pitched
in to prepare supper the Capt. taking
an active part & proving a jovial
helpmate. After disposing of what
sowb (elly) & bread we had & as all hands
were backed up warming their backs
legs & spinal columns. We com (menced)
joking Steve upon the prospect
of having to assist in carrying the
boxes to the top of the mesa, to photo
some houses, not dreaming our
selves than any were really there.
He asked us to point out the
spot. The Capt. pointed at
random. "Yes" says he "I see it".
I beheld upon my close observation
their was something that appeared
very like a house. The doors &
windows could be seen. We all
started at once to investigate.
The side of the Canon was formed
of successive tables or benches of Sandstone
rising perpendicularly one above
the other to a total height of
about 800 feet. Our house
was upon the last one & below
it the precipice was fully 100
feet above the narrow bench at
(its foot.)

Mesa Verde — Cliff Palace

Mesa Verde — Cliff Palace from the inside

62

Mesa Verde — cliff dwellings in Mancos Canon

Relics from the cliff dwellings in Mancos Canon

On the trail to the cliff dwellings in Mancos Canon

← Mesa Verde — Square Tower

Mesa Verde — The Sandal House in Mancos Canon

Mesa Verde — cliff dwellings in Mancos Canon

The Hovenweep Castle on the Hovenweep River — 1874

Ouray, Chief of the Uncompahgre Utes — August 19, 1874

Chipeta, wife of Chief Ouray — August 19, 1874

Ruins of Chief Ouray's house

Ignacio, Chief of the Southern Utes

Peah, a chief of the Uncompahgre Utes — 1874

Buckskin Charlie, Ute Sub-Chief

The children of Severo, Chief of the Capote Utes

Ute Indians at the National Mining and Industrial Exposition in Denver — 1882

Wagon Wheels to Steel Rails

The progress of America's westward movement was determined in large part by the development of the nation's transportation systems. The first wave of pioneers utilized the slow but sturdy Conestoga Wagon, hauled by patient oxen. Later the frontier settlements were connected by networks of horse-drawn stage coaches and freight wagons. However, the vast resources of the new land remained largely untapped. The mineral wealth, timber, products of farm and ranch, all awaited a catalyst for development. A viable mode of transportation was on the horizon and heading west on shining rails: the railroad era was about to explode in Colorado and the West as the 1870's approached.

William Henry Jackson was keenly aware of the role of the iron horse in the "winning of the West", for he had spent the summer of 1869 fulfilling a contract with the Union Pacific Railroad to photograph along their newly completed transcontinental line across Wyoming and Utah. Thus it was that when Jackson decided, in 1879, to open a studio in Denver and to specialize in scenic photography, he began at once to seek work with the railroads which were then in the midst of laying rails at a feverish rate in a race to reach each new mining camp and also provide a through line across the Rockies from Denver.

The railroads were eager to be photographed, perhaps for the record it would provide for company property files, but more importantly as part of their advertising program to lure passengers and to assure freight shippers of the high standards of their trackage and equipment. Jackson was usually provided a private train, allowing the expedition to remain on the tour for several days while living in comfortable accommodations, with ample storage for photographic equipment and supplies. The one or two-car special train appears in many of his photographs, posed while the photographic crew located a vantage point suitable to Jackson's exacting requirements.

Jackson's first Colorado railroad work was in 1881, for the Denver & Rio Grande Railway, followed soon by an assignment from the Denver, South Park & Pacific Railroad. He photographed the Colorado Midland in 1888, and during the early 1890's covered both the Rio Grande Southern Railway and the unique cog line of the Manitou & Pike's Peak Railway.

Jackson obtained many of his finest photographs while working for the railroads and they provided much of his stock of sales material well into the Twentieth Century. They provide us today with not only a record of railroad operations in that era, but just as importantly, the scenic locales and towns along the routes.

Cog train at Halfway House, Manitou & Pike's Peak Ry.

In the Royal Gorge at the Hanging Bridge, D.&R.G. Ry.

Water stop at Windy Point, Manitou & Pike's Peak Ry.

The last glimpse of Cascade — Pike's Peak tollroad

July snowstorm on Pike's Peak

Observatory and shelter house at the summit of Pike's Peak

On the road to Cripple Creek

Stage arrival at Fremont, Cripple Creek District

St. Peter's Dome, Colorado Springs & Cripple Creek District Ry.

Mt. Shavano from Poncha Pass, Denver & Rio Grande Ry.

Ascending Marshall Pass above Mears, Denver & Rio Grande Ry.

Climbing Marshall Pass, Denver & Rio Grande Ry.

Mt. Ouray and Marshall Pass, Denver & Rio Grande Ry.

Passenger train climbing west side of Marshall Pass, D.& R.G.Ry.

Work train on west side of Marshall Pass, Denver & Rio Grande Ry.

88

Black Canon of the Gunnison at Bridge "B", D.&R.G.Ry.

Chipeta Falls in the Black Canon of the Gunnison, D.&R.G. Ry.

Near Wild Horse along the Arkansas River on the Colorado Midland Ry.

90

High bridge near Buena Vista on the Colorado Midland Ry.

A panorama of the east side of Hagerman Pass, Colorado Midland Ry.

Snowplow at Ivanhoe, Colorado Midland Ry.

The high bridge in the Georgetown Loop, looking west, Colorado Central R.R.

The Georgetown Loop high bridge from above, Colorado Central R.R.

London Junction, Denver, South Park & Pacific R.R.

The Georgetown Loop looking east toward Georgetown, Colorado Central R.R. — 1884

Fremont Pass, Denver & Rio Grande Ry. and Denver, South Park & Pacific R.R.

Descending from Alpine Tunnel, Denver, South Park & Pacific R.R.

On Alpine Pass, Denver, South Park & Pacific R.R.

In April, 1890, the Denver, South Park & Pacific R.R. decided to test the newly developed Jull Centrifugal Snow Excavator, as a possible answer to their snow removal problems, and Jackson was retained to photograph the "trials". The Jull plow (above) with its huge auger proved cumbersome and after it became mired down several times, the line's rotary snow plow proved to be superior by easily clearing the track.

Rear view of rotary on its way to victory — April 18, 1890

Rotary starting in where Jull plow failed — April 16, 1890

White Rock Point between Cumbres, Colorado and Chama, New Mexico, D.&R.G.Ry.

Phantom Curve, east of Cumbres Pass on the Denver & Rio Grande Ry.

La Veta Pass and Dump Mountain, Denver & Rio Grande Ry.

Canon of the Rio Los Animas, Denver & Rio Grande Ry.

Mt. Abram from the Ouray and Silverton Toll Road

Rockwood in the Canon of the Rio Los Animas, Denver & Rio Grande Ry.

Toll gate between Ouray and Silverton

Burros packed for the mountains, a street scene in Ouray

Departure of stages from Dolores.

Lizard Head, Rio Grande Southern Ry.

Coal breaker and mine, Anthracite Mesa, Crested Butte

114

Lure of the High Country

Of all of the Jackson photographs of Colorado, none are more fascinating, nor more vital for the record they provide, than those of the towns and mining camps which sprang up and flourished during his time. The gold and silver strikes were largely responsible for the rapid pace of exploration and development in Colorado. But with the ores long since exhausted and mining unprofitable due to changes in the national economy, the handiwork of man has proven very fragile. The bustling towns and giant mining complexes which appeared both prosperous and permanent before Jackson's camera, have more often than not all but vanished from the face of the earth.

His particular ability to place the essence of a spectacular scene on glass plate or film, enabled Jackson to reflect in his pictures the vastness of nature as compared to man's undertakings. Time and again his photos place an impressive mining operation, or a flourishing town into prospective as a rather minor part of a panoramic scene in the Rockies, a viewpoint sometimes difficult for man to accept.

A select few pioneer towns and mining camps have spanned the change in economic fortunes and become the cities of Western Colorado. Here, as with the Front Range cities, we are offered a rare opportunity to see the changes wrought by what has now been nearly a century since Jackson passed this way.

Elkton Mine, Cripple Creek

Buena Vista Mine and Pike's Peak

A pioneer merchant in Fremont, the Cripple Creek District

Cripple Creek panorama

Silver Plume

Georgetown from Leavenworth Mountain

Idaho Springs

Central City

Caribou, Boulder County

Alma, Park County

Mines of Battle Mountain, Eagle River Canon

Gilman and the Eagle River Canon

Redcliff, Eagle County

Altman, the highest city in America, 10,620 feet

Leadville from Capitol Hill

The Leadville Ice Palace, 1895

Colonel Sellers Mine in California Gulch, Leadville

The Little Pittsburgh Mine, Leadville

The Hotel Colorado, Glenwood Springs

Glenwood Springs looking south across the Grand (Colorado) River

The Glenwood Hot Springs Pool and bath house

Aspen and Aspen Mountain

Spring Gulch Coal Mine and Mt. Sopris

The Lixivator Smelter, Aspen

The Arkansas River, Salida and the Sawatch Range

139

The La Veta Hotel, Gunnison

Ranching at Cimarron on the Gunnison River

Cimarron on the Gunnison River, Denver & Rio Grande Ry.

Panorama of Upper Creede

Upper Creede

Panorama of Durango

Creede Avenue in Lower Creede

Red Mountain Mine near Ouray

Gold mining in Borens Gulch, La Plata County — 1875

Silverton and Sultan Mountain

Yankee Girl Mine along the Silverton Railroad

Sheridan Mine Incline at Pandora

Ouray and the San Juan Mountains

Telluride, Main Street

Burros hauling timber for the mines, Ouray

Denver, 16th and Curtis Streets

156

Gateways to the Rockies

William Henry Jackson was primarily a scenic photographer. He had a lifelong goal to capture in photographs the natural wonders of America as they appeared in the closing decades of the Nineteenth Century. One suspects he must have sensed the urgency of his task as the untouched wilderness yielded to the advances of civilization.

Occasionally, perhaps to satisfy his customers and to lend a balance to his catalog of offerings, he included exposures of the towns and cities he visited on his photographic expeditions. In addition, he made an extensive series of shots in and around Denver, providing us with a fine record of the city as it was growing from a small frontier town to take its place as the metropolis of the Intermountain West.

Jackson's capacity for capturing the natural scene is reflected in his use of panoramic photographs to include the full majesty and scenic qualities of a town or city. This technique is reflected in his photo of Colorado Springs at the foot of towering Pike's Peak and in such scenes as Golden, nestled at the base of North and South Table Mountains. Jackson often used two or three slightly overlapping photographs to provide an especially wide panorama and carried this technique to its ultimate with a six photo panorama of Denver.

Jackson has provided us with a rare glimpse of the front range cities in their young and robust state, a sharp contrast to the megalopolis which is forecast to span the length of the front range by the end of this century.

Pueblo, looking northeast past the Union Depot

Miners' dugout

Manitou on the Colorado Midland Ry.

Colorado Springs and Pike's Peak

The Broadmoor Casino, Colorado Springs

Boulder, looking southwest toward the Flatirons

Boulder, looking west to Long's Peak

Note: The above photo is rather unique, since there is no location in Boulder which would present this view of Long's Peak. One can only speculate as to how Jackson managed to achieve the end result.

A bit of Estes Park from the stage window

The Robber's Roost — stage station and former outlaw hangout, Virginia Dale — 1870

Golden, looking east between North and South Table Mountains

A panorama of yesterday! Denver at the close of the 19th century

Platte Canyon with irrigation flume, south of Denver

168

Denver, the 16th Street Viaduct and downtown

The gold-domed Colorado capitol, circa 1900

Denver Union Station at the turn of the century

170

Denver City Hall, 1886

The Mining Exchange Building, topped by the bronze miner

University Hall, "Old Main," University of Denver, 1891

The text for this book was photo-composed by Sand Creek Type Company, Lakewood, Colorado, using an eleven point Century typeface, with three points of space between the lines. Display type is Windsor Bold. Offset lithography was by Pruett Press/O'Hara Corp., Boulder, Colorado, using an eighty pound Mead Offset Gloss Enamel for the text and one hundred pound Tiara Vicksburg Vellum Text on the endpapers.

Edition binding was by Roswell Bookbinding, Phoenix, Arizona.